Forever Flames and Twisted Trees

Forever Flames and Twisted Trees

Abbie Rushton

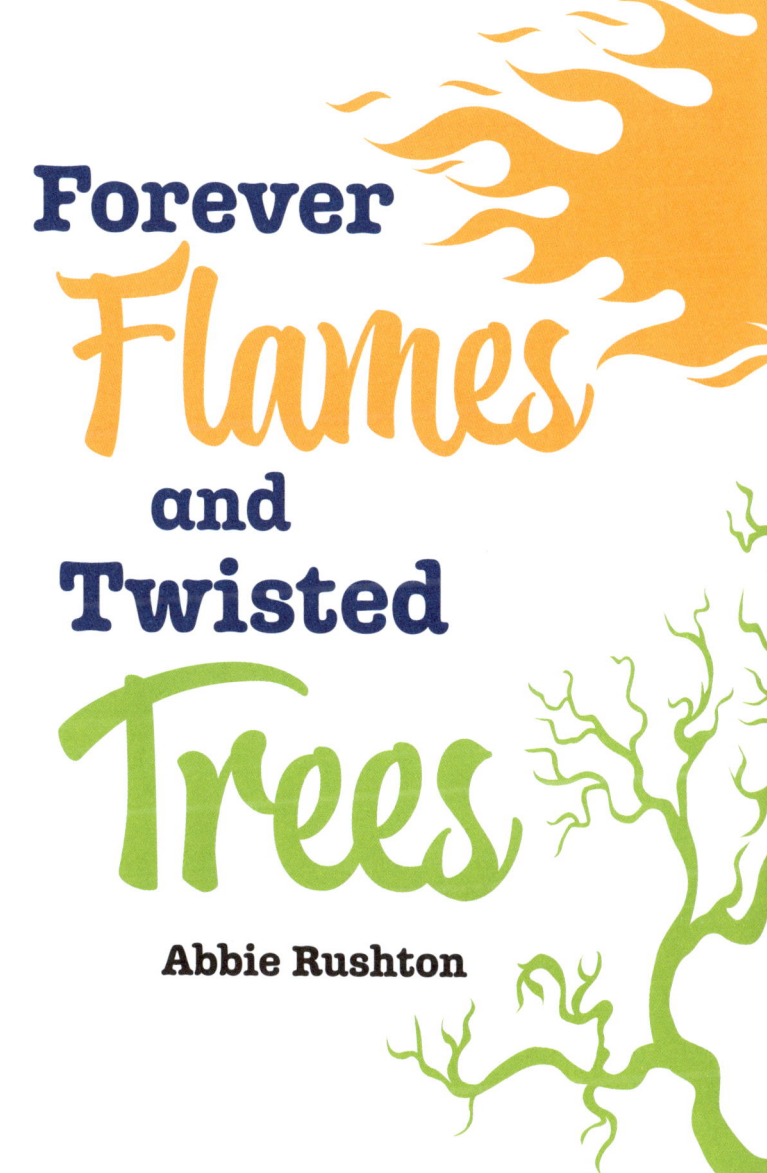

Collins

Contents

Bonus: Where are we going?............ 2

Chapter 1 Wondrous water 4

Bonus: Brilliant bioluminescence!....... 14

Chapter 2 Fantastic forests............ 16

Chapter 3 Cool caves 26

Chapter 4 Magnificent mountains....... 34

Bonus: Plan a mountain expedition!..... 42

Chapter 5 Dazzling deserts 44

Bonus: Investigating the Nazca lines..... 54

Chapter 6 Beautiful beaches 56

Bonus: Packing list.................. 66

Glossary.......................... 68

About the author 70

Book chat.......................... 72

Bonus
Where are we going?

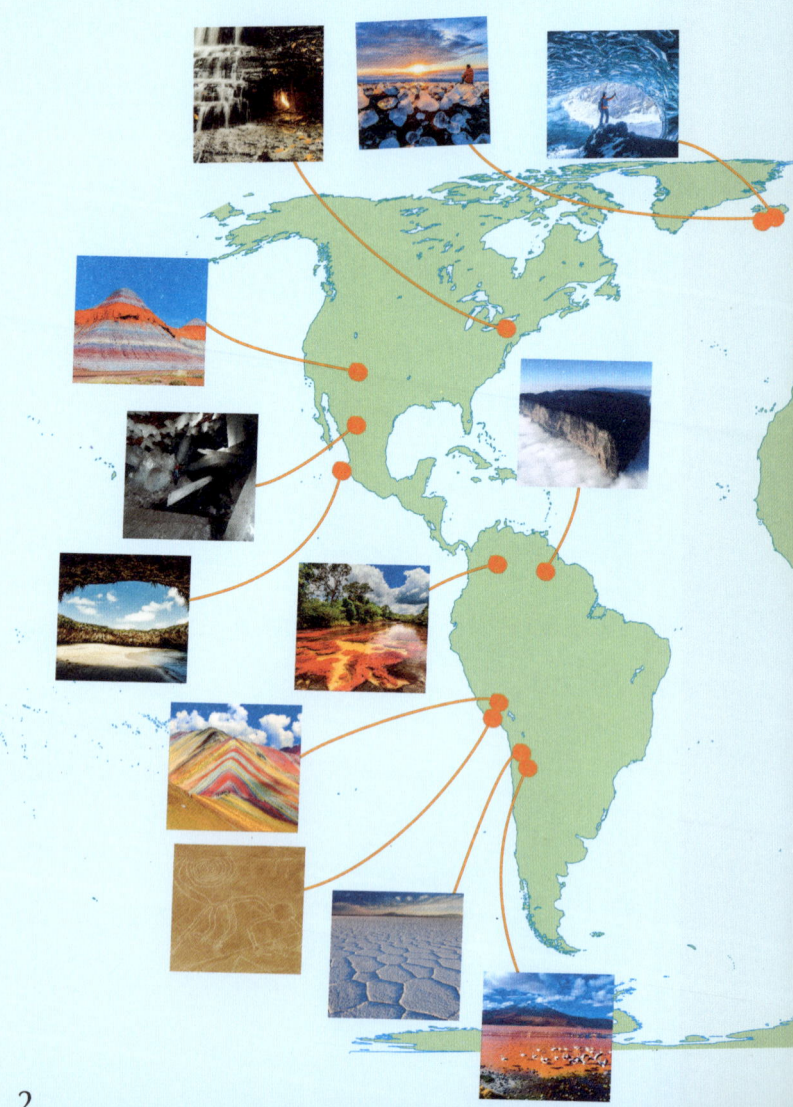

2

We will explore some amazing places in this book! Let's see which parts of our incredible world we are going to learn about ...

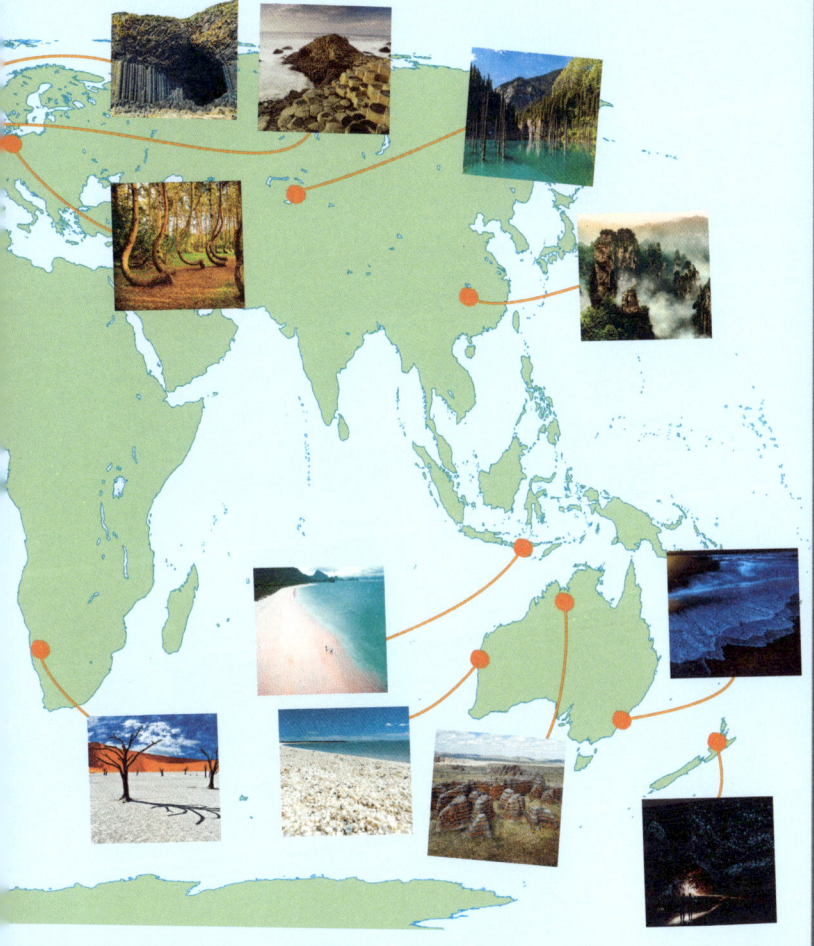

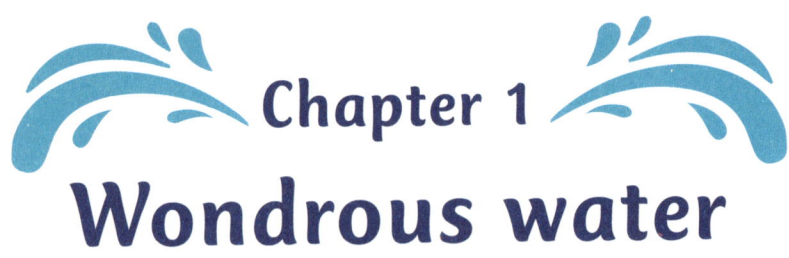

Chapter 1
Wondrous water

Let's explore some amazing places

This book will guide you to some of the most unique places in the world. From eerie forests to a huge salt plain, and from mysterious mountains to a rainbow river, let's take a closer look at our wonderful world!

First, let's look at some rare sights in our rivers and seas. We know that over two-thirds of the world's surface is covered by water, so there's lots to explore.

The River of Five Colours, Colombia

This stunning river is one of South America's most impressive natural wonders. Some people call it a 'liquid rainbow' because of the beautiful palette of colours. You can often see greens, yellows, reds, pinks and purples. These vibrant colours come from a plant which is unique to Colombia.

When to go

If you visit at the wrong time of year, you'll be disappointed. The plant only blooms in the period between Colombia's wet and dry seasons. In the wet season, the river is too high, so the sun doesn't reach the plants. In the dry season, there isn't enough water for the plants to grow. The best time to go is around July to November.

The Eternal Flame Falls, New York state, USA

Picture this: you're in the United States, not far from the world-famous Niagara Falls waterfall. However, you are heading towards a much smaller, less well-known waterfall. You trek along a stream bed, with beautiful woodland **ravines** all around you.

Then you catch a glimpse of the reason you're here: the Eternal Flame Falls. This seems to go against the laws of science: a burning flame in the middle of a waterfall!

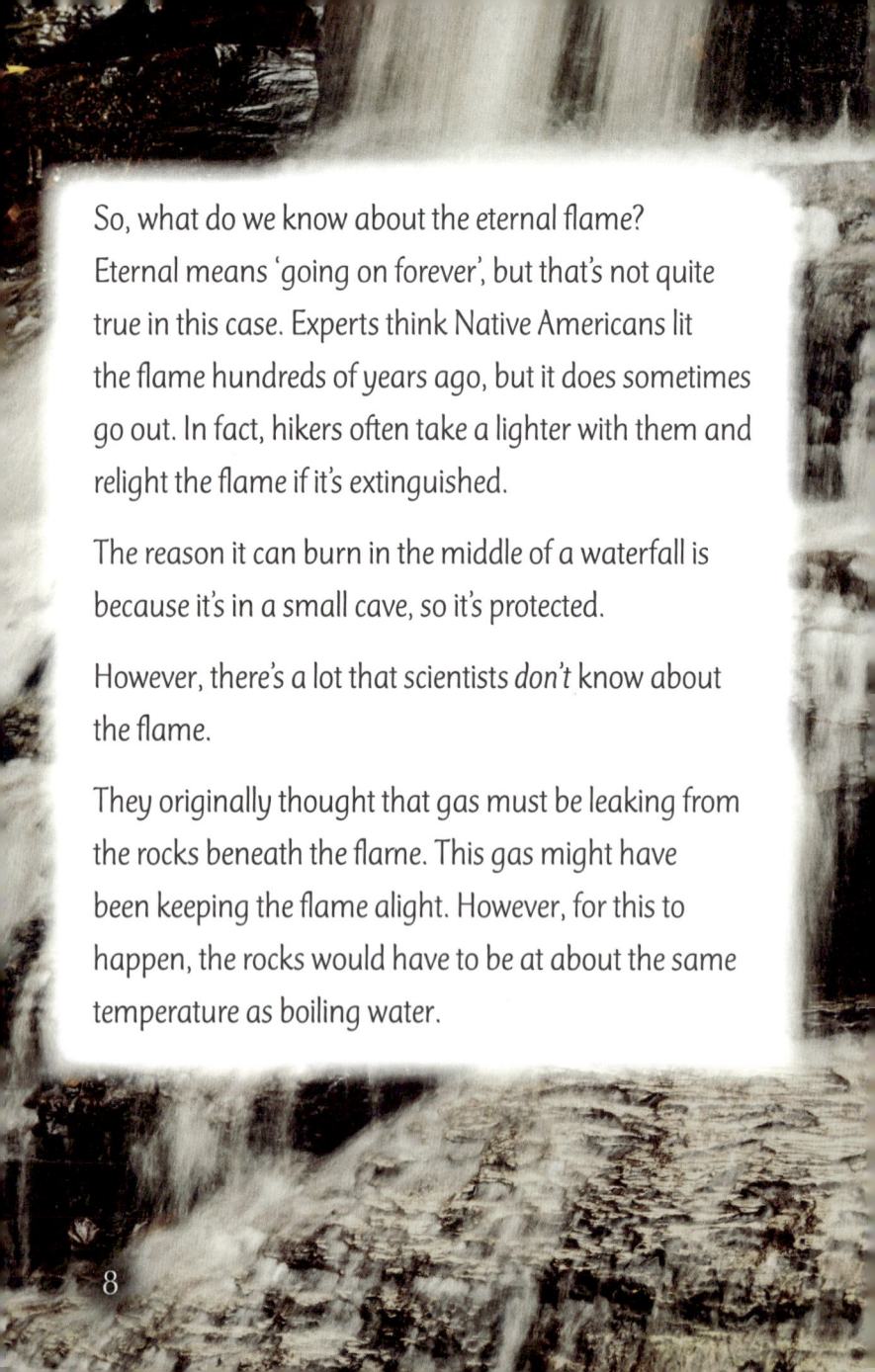

So, what do we know about the eternal flame? Eternal means 'going on forever', but that's not quite true in this case. Experts think Native Americans lit the flame hundreds of years ago, but it does sometimes go out. In fact, hikers often take a lighter with them and relight the flame if it's extinguished.

The reason it can burn in the middle of a waterfall is because it's in a small cave, so it's protected.

However, there's a lot that scientists *don't* know about the flame.

They originally thought that gas must be leaking from the rocks beneath the flame. This gas might have been keeping the flame alight. However, for this to happen, the rocks would have to be at about the same temperature as boiling water.

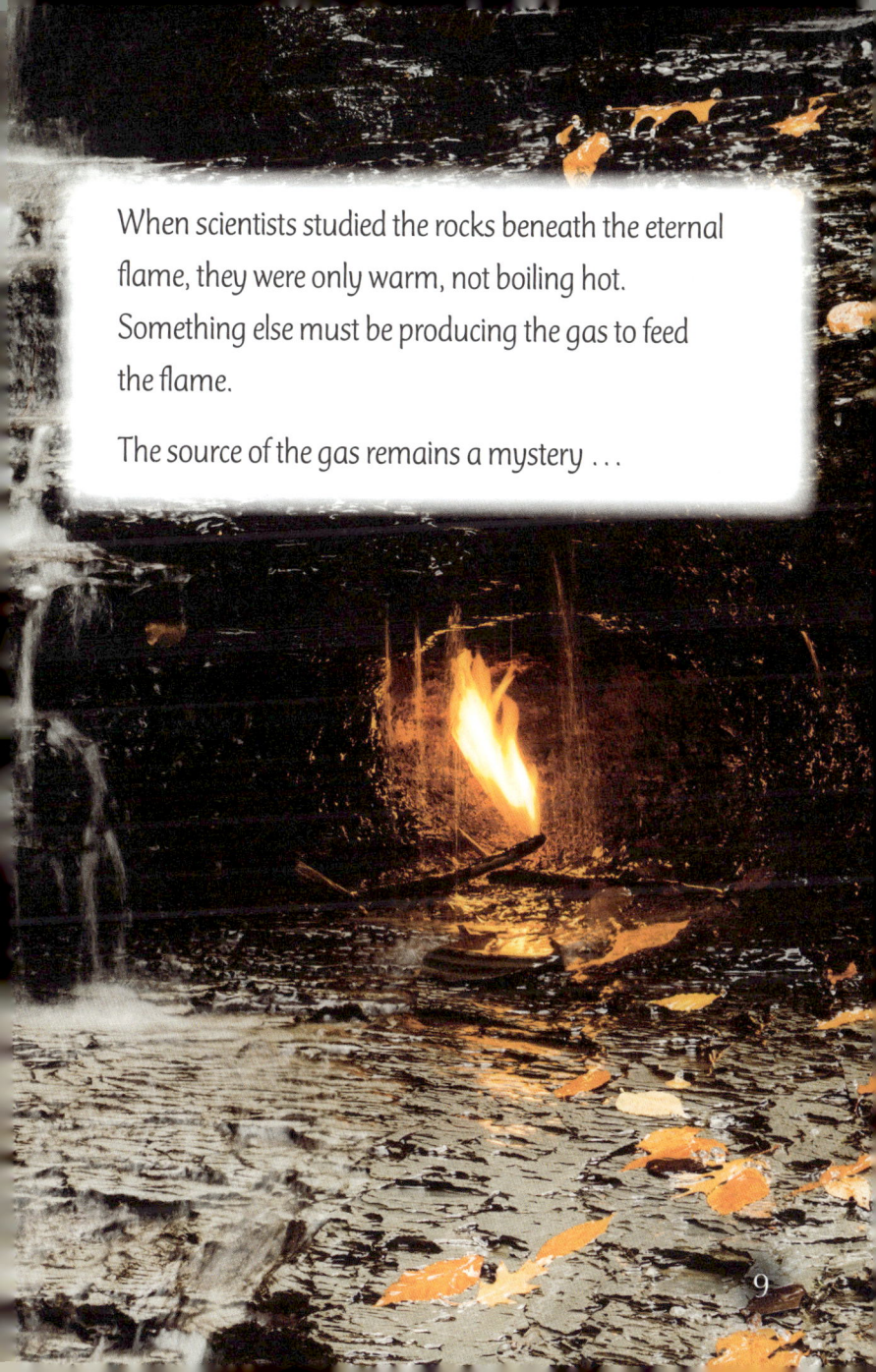

When scientists studied the rocks beneath the eternal flame, they were only warm, not boiling hot. Something else must be producing the gas to feed the flame.

The source of the gas remains a mystery ...

When to go

The best time to see the flame is September to May, when there's lots of water. This is because the water protects the flame from wind, which might extinguish it.

If you visit during the winter months, you may be rewarded with an even more spectacular sight. You might see a burning flame in the middle of a glistening, frozen waterfall!

Bioluminescence, Jervis Bay, Australia

This experience is not for you if you're afraid of the dark! However, if you're happy to venture out at night, you can see one of nature's true wonders: bioluminescence. It can make the water seem blue, green and sometimes even red!

> **? What is bioluminescence?**
> Bioluminescence is tiny living creatures producing their own light. Tiny **marine** creatures, called plankton, produce bioluminescence in the sea.

Bioluminescence happens when there is movement in the water. For example, a wave might have a shimmering crest of bioluminescence, or a boat oar might leave a gleaming trail.

If you throw rocks into some water, you may see bioluminescent splashes.

What is bioluminescence for?
Experts think that bioluminescence could help living creatures catch prey, defend themselves against attack or find a mate.

So how can you see bioluminescence? Sadly, it's very hard to predict and you can never guarantee that you'll see it. In Jervis Bay, it's more common in the warmer months, especially after rain. This is because the rain adds **nutrients** to the water, which help the plankton to glow.

Fact!

Plankton that produce bioluminescence can tell whether it's day or night! They only light up at night. Scientists tested this by putting some plankton in a dark place during daytime, but the plankton weren't fooled. They didn't start making bioluminescence!

Bonus
Brilliant bioluminescence!

Ghost fungi

Location: Australia

Comb jelly

Location: USA and Canada

Glow-worms

Location: glow-worm cave in New Zealand

Sea slugs

Location: across the world

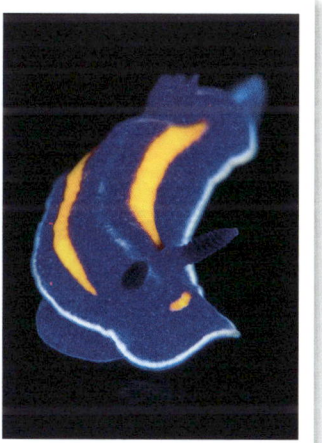

Coral

Location: across the world

Chapter 2
Fantastic forests

Dead Marsh, Namibia

Most of us quite enjoy a stroll in a wood. However, you might not be so keen to wander through some of these creepy forests!

Our first forest even has a ghostly name that means 'Dead Marsh'. 'Dead' refers to the skeletons of the camel thorn trees, which died around 900 years ago.

Let's set the scene. Dead Marsh is in the middle of the Namib desert, surrounded by towering fiery-coloured sand dunes. The trees grow out of stark white clay. Their branches reach up like fingers towards the sky, as if they are begging for water.

> Can you spot the person?
> Some of these sand dunes are among the highest in the world!

To find out what created this unique sight, we need to go back in time …

Experts think the marsh formed over 1,000 years ago, when the river overflowed in the rainy season. The trees grew in the wet ground. However, due to changes in weather and shifting sand dunes blocking off the river, the water dried up.

The trees died, but they didn't rot because the air was too dry. The clay dried up, became solid and held the trees in place.

When to go

As you'd expect in a desert, daytime temperatures can get extremely hot. Therefore, it's best to visit Dead Marsh in the early morning or late afternoon. The light then is perfect for some amazing photographs of the trees' silhouettes.

What else is there to see?

If you're feeling energetic, you could tackle 'Big Daddy'! This is a massive sand dune near Dead Marsh. It's amazing to look out across the desert from the top.

The Crooked Forest, Poland

Now let's delve into another unsolved mystery! If you visit this forest in Poland, you'll come across some incredibly unusual pine trees. They all grow in the same strange bent shape, and nobody knows why!

Let's look at the facts.

- The trees were planted in the late 1920s and early 1930s.
- Something happened to the trees when they were 7–10 years old to make them grow this way.
- After the Second World War started in 1939, the local town of Gryfino was deserted. So the people who planted the trees left and took their secrets with them …

There are various explanations for the trees' strange shapes.

Here are some of them.

Explanation 1
A heavy snowfall covered the trees and affected their growth. However, this can't be true because there are trees in the same forest which don't grow this strange way.

Explanation 2
Local people made the trees grow this way. When the trees are young, it's easy to bend and shape them. Then they could be used to make curved wooden items like furniture or musical instruments.

Explanation 3

The trees were flattened and damaged by German tanks during the Second World War.

Explanation 4

The trees fell over, perhaps because of a storm. They tried to get themselves in the right position by altering their trunks to grow upwards.

The truth is, we may never know why the trees grow like this. What do you think the reason is?

Kaindy Lake, Central Asia

You should stop to breathe in the fresh mountain air at this beautiful lake. You would probably admire the incredible blue water or the lush green of the surrounding mountains. However, you might be surprised to see some spruce trees which appear to grow straight out of the lake!

Sadly, a bit like Dead Marsh, the trees are now dead. Some people think the trees look the masts of ghost ships. What do you think?

Not many people visit this amazing mountain lake, as other lakes close by are easier to reach. If you do go there, you can look down into the clear water and see the spruces' dead branches.

However, some people have dived into the water to see and photograph the strange underwater forest.

So how did this peculiar sight come about? There's a clue in the name of the lake! It means 'falling rocks' or 'landslide lake'.

In 1911, there was an earthquake. The fallen rocks created a dam, which trapped the water. The trees died in the water, but simply stayed where they were. Due to the cold temperatures, they haven't rotted, and they have remained there for over 100 years.

Chapter 3
Cool caves

Fingal's Cave, Scotland

Let's start with a cave that you need to make a special effort to visit. Fingal's Cave is on an island which you can only reach by boat. You can see the cave from the sea. You can see the cave from the sea, or you can land on the island and walk to the cave.

This beautiful cave is made from a series of hexagonal columns. The rock is basalt, which is cooled **lava**.

Fingal's Cave

There are many myths and legends surrounding Fingal's Cave. In fact, its name comes from a legendary Irish warrior often known as Finn MacCool. Legend has it that Finn made the Giant's Causeway in Northern Ireland, which are giant columns that look like stepping-stones in the sea.

There is some truth in the link between Fingal's Cave and the Giant's Causeway. Both of these incredible natural wonders were formed by lava that came from the same volcano millions of years ago! Experts think there may have been a 'bridge' between Fingal's Cave and the Giant's Causeway.

Giant's Causeway

The cave has inspired artists and musicians. In fact, a piece of classical music made the cave popular with tourists. The piece, called *Fingal's Cave*, was written after the composer visited in 1829.

Queen Victoria and Prince Albert visited in 1847, and a stream of famous poets, painters and writers have also been to see this incredible sight.

What else is there to see?

Another popular activity on this island is puffin spotting. These colourful birds nest on the cliffs of the island.

tourists visiting Fingal's Cave

Glacier Caves, Iceland

You'd need to wrap up warm for the next caves. That's because you'd be going inside a glacier – a huge piece of ice. And not just any glacier – one of the largest in the world!

You must go with a guide, as it would be extremely dangerous to go alone. The guide would give you the correct gear, including a helmet. You'd also need crampons. These fix to the bottom of your shoes. They have spikes to stop you from slipping on the snow and ice.

How do the caves form?

Every summer, some of the glacier water melts. This makes caves inside the glacier. You can only visit these caves in the winter, when all the ice around the caves has frozen solid again.

Because of the way they are formed, the caves pop up in different places each year. They are also totally unique and even change each day! For example, they might melt a bit and change size slightly. Or the colour might look different on different days.

Giant Crystal Cave, Mexico

This cave is beneath a mountain in Mexico. A mining company has been taking out metal from the mines for hundreds of years. However, in 2000, two brothers who worked for the mining company made an extraordinary discovery.

They found a cave full of enormous crystals. These are some of the largest crystals ever discovered, and some are longer than a bus!

You might expect caves to be dark, wet and cold. The Giant Crystal Cave is two of those things, but it's certainly not cold! In fact, it's incredibly hot – too hot for humans to spend much time there.

It's also humid, which means there's a lot of water in the air. This makes it really hard to breathe.

At first, researchers could only go in the caves for periods of five minutes. Any longer would cause serious damage to their bodies. Then scientists developed special suits packed with ice, which meant they could go down for 30–45 minutes.

Scientist Penny Boston describes what it was like:

> "I could feel the strength draining from my arms and legs, and movement growing harder and harder [...] My temper was unusually short."

How did the crystals form?

The Giant Crystal Cave is inside a mountain that was formed by a volcano 26 million years ago. The cave was filled with hot water which was full of **minerals**. It was kept warm from **magma** from the volcano beneath it. As the water cooled, the minerals formed into crystals. Scientists think they took around one million years to grow.

The caves are now closed and have been allowed to flood again. Just picture how big the crystals might be if someone discovers them again in hundreds, or even thousands, of years!

Chapter 4
Magnificent mountains

Tianzi Mountain Nature Reserve, China

If you take the cable car up China's Tianzi (say "Tee-an-zee") Mountain, you'll be rewarded with a beautiful sight. These incredible peaks are often veiled in a ghostly mist, giving them an air of mystery. They almost look as if they are floating, rising up from the clouds. These straight, narrow stone columns are covered with lush greenery.

Surrounding the peaks is an area of outstanding natural beauty, full of forests, waterfalls, caves, rivers and wildlife.

These mountains may look as if they could topple at any minute. However, experts think that they've been there for around 400 million years!

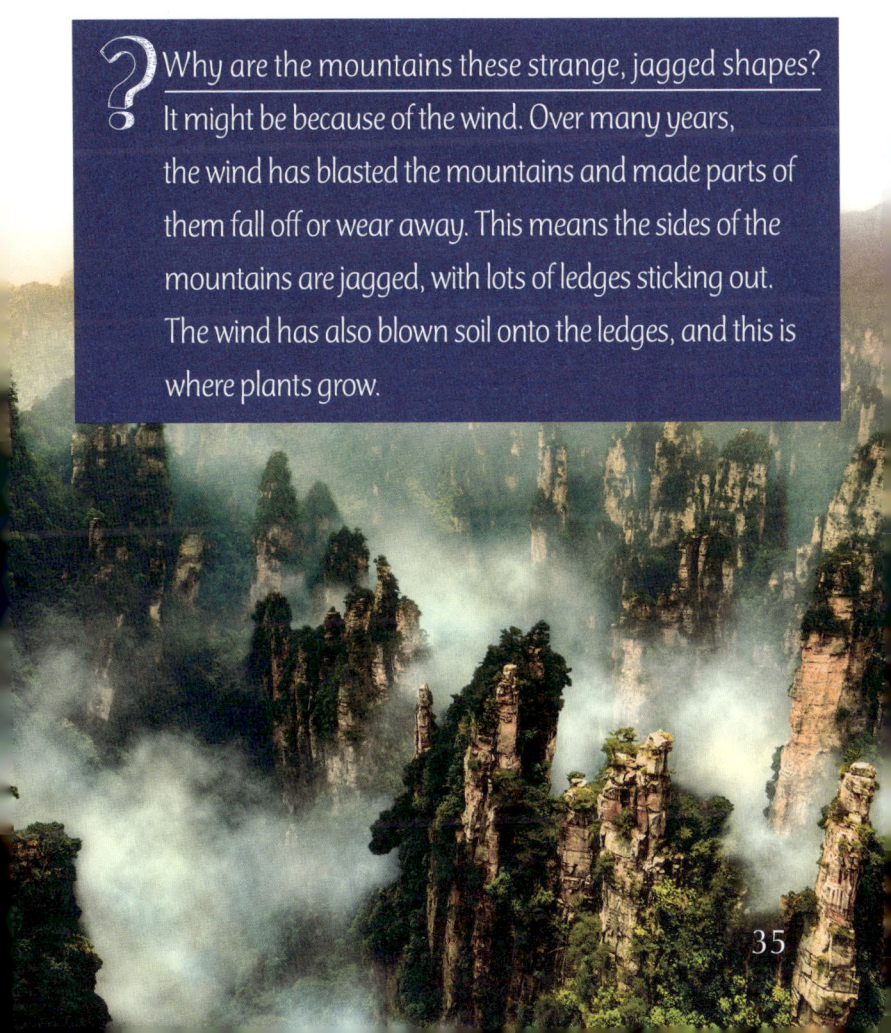

> **Why are the mountains these strange, jagged shapes?**
> It might be because of the wind. Over many years, the wind has blasted the mountains and made parts of them fall off or wear away. This means the sides of the mountains are jagged, with lots of ledges sticking out. The wind has also blown soil onto the ledges, and this is where plants grow.

Rainbow Mountain, Peru

This is perhaps one of the most recently discovered places in the book. The mountain only became visible in 2013 because it was previously covered in snow. When the snow melted, this stunning collage of colours could be seen. The amazing colours are created by different minerals in the earth.

When to go

Rainbow Mountain is around 5,000 metres above sea level, so the weather can be unpredictable. The best time to see it is in Peru's dry season, which is April to October.

Also, the time of day that you visit can affect the colours that you'll see. On clear, sunny days, the colours will seem much brighter.

Be warned: you'll need a very early start to see Rainbow Mountain! It's a long, winding road from the nearest tourist town, Cusco, and the drive takes about three hours. Then it's a difficult trek to get close to the mountain. Because it's so high up, the air is thin and hard to breathe.

Bungle Bungle mountain range, Australia

You might think the next range of mountains is a **mirage**. The Bungle Bungle mountains rise up from the middle of a desert like a series of beehives.

These mountains are a long way from any town. Most of the world only found out about them in the 1980s. Before that, only local people knew about them. A film crew was making a documentary in the area and flew over the mountains. Since they were included in the documentary, the mountains have become more famous!

These mountains may win a prize for the most interesting name! However, no one seems to know where the name came from. There is no such word in the language of the First Nation Australians who live in the area.

There is something else that makes the area around the Bungle Bungle mountains special. In 2013, an astronaut took a picture of the mountains from space. Scientists believe it shows a **meteorite crater** that was formed between 180 and 300 million years ago, when a large meteorite hit Earth.

crater

How were the mountains formed?
They were made from layers of rock that have been squashed together and then worn away by the wind. The dark grey veins and layers are made by a kind of **bacteria** living in the rock.

Island in the Clouds

This is one of the oldest mountains on the planet! It could be about two billion years old. For comparison, Mount Everest is only about 60 million years old.

This mountain sits on the border of three South American countries. If you made the trek, you could explore the massive flat top. It's known as a 'table-top' mountain.

Picture yourself there now. You're surrounded by a sea of mist, so it feels as though the mysterious mountain is floating on the clouds. There are sheer 400-metre cliffs plunging down before you. It rains almost daily here, and you can hear the roar of a waterfall. The water plummets over the top, disappearing into the mist.

What else is there to see?

About one third of the plants and animals on this mountain are unique to this place. That means they don't live anywhere else.

This pitcher plant gobbles up insects.

You'd have to look very carefully to spot this tiny toad.

Bonus
Plan a mountain expedition!

Gear

Things to pack:

- rucksack with waterproof covering
- ice pick
- crampons
- climbing harness and ropes
- head torch
- thermal sleeping bag
- tent
- food and water
- first-aid kit
- map and compass

Top tips

1. Make a plan – How far can you walk each day and where will you camp? Share this plan with someone else so they know where you're going to be.

2. Check the weather often – Do you have what you need for all weathers?

3. Pack food and water – Do you have all you need? Pack extra, just in case.

4. Have the right team – Do you have people with you who are experienced climbers?

Chapter 5
Dazzling deserts

The Nazca Lines, Peru

The Nazca Lines are a series of large designs that have been carved into the ground in a desert in Peru. They are pictures of plants, animals and other shapes. The pictures are so big that you have to fly over them to see them fully.

the monkey

the spider

How were the Nazca lines formed?

Experts believe the lines were made by the Nazca people, who lived over 1,000 years ago. They created the lines by scraping off the top layer of rust-coloured pebbles to reveal the white sand beneath.

Why have the Nazca lines stayed like this for such a long time?

The desert is dry, with not much wind or rain, which means the lines have not been disturbed.

There are lots of ideas about why the Nazca lines were created. The most popular idea is that the pictures were a way to ask the gods for things like food or water.

Some experts think that monkeys and spiders were symbols of rain for the Nazca people. So perhaps they made pictures of these animals to ask the gods for rain during dry periods.

The hummingbird was a sign of life and growth. A hummingbird picture might be a way to ask for healthy crops and food to eat.

the hummingbird

Salt desert, Bolivia

If someone asked you to picture a desert, you would probably think of sand. However, this desert is made of salt!

Around 40,000 years ago, this area was covered by a saltwater lake. When the water dried up, it just left the salt — ten billion tons of it! This is the largest salt desert on the planet.

When to go

The choice is yours! If you go in the rainy season between December and April, you can walk across the wet salt. It's like walking on a mirror! However, in the dry season, which is May to November, you can drive across the salt flats because the ground is hard. This means you might be able to explore areas that you can't reach in the rainy season.

What else is there to see?

Your tour might also stop at Laguna Colorada, which means 'red lagoon' in the local language. This lake is impressive for two reasons: the incredible colour, and the flocks of bright pink flamingos that come here.

The red colour of the lake comes from living things and sediment (little bits of rock or soil) in the water.

Painted Desert, Arizona, USA

Picture yourself in a hot, dry desert, looking at this beautiful palette of colours. You'll see reds, yellows, blues, purples and white. Sometimes, even the air looks pink or purple as dust gets blown in the wind.

In the Painted Desert, the colour of the soil looks different, depending on the position of the sun. This is a unique and ever-changing place.

The Painted Desert is a place with a mixture of soft and hard rocks, and clay soil. The softer rocks and clay got worn away over time. The hard rocks were left. This created interesting shapes such as canyons and ravines.

Some of the rock shapes are about 200 million years old. Because there were lots of volcanoes in this area, some of the rocks have a layer of volcanic ash on top.

What else is there to see?

In one corner of the Painted Desert, people flock to see another incredible natural wonder. Some ancient wood here has turned into a stone called quartz.

Over 200 million years ago, some trees were washed into a river. They were so deep under the water that it took hundreds of years for them to **decay**. Over time, the wood slowly absorbed chemicals from the water. The chemicals **crystallised**, turning the logs into quartz stone.

What else is there to see?

You can't miss the *enormous* tourist attraction that draws most people to this area: the Grand Canyon! It's about a four hour drive away from the Painted Desert.

The Grand Canyon is so famous, you might think we know a lot about it. In fact, no one is sure how old it is. People used to think that the canyon was made about six million years ago. However, scientists now think it may have been as many as 70 million years ago!

Bonus
Investigating the Nazca lines

No one really knows what the Nazca lines are for. Here are some different ideas.

A calendar
One opinion is that the lines were the largest calendar in the world.

Aliens
Another idea is that aliens visited the Nazca people. After the aliens left, the Nazca people made the images as messages to the aliens.

Some people think this picture, known as 'the astronaut' may show an alien.

A racetrack

Some people suggest that the lines might be a special sort of racetrack for the Nazca people.

Important pathways

One opinion is that the lines were walking tracks which were used during religious ceremonies.

Water markers

Some people think that the lines showed where water could be found underground.

What do you think?

Chapter 6
Beautiful beaches

Hidden Beach, Mexico

Picture yourself lying on the sand on this secret and sheltered beach. The earth almost seems to wrap around you, hiding you from people above.

You'd have taken quite a trip to get there. This unique wonder lies on the **uninhabited** Marietas Island. First, there's an hour-long boat ride. Then you have to either swim or row a boat through a long, narrow tunnel.

The island was formed when an underwater volcano erupted thousands of years ago. The Hidden Beach might look as if it's in a volcano crater — but is it? Over 100 years ago, weapons were tested on the island. Maybe a bomb made the crater above the Hidden Beach?

Pink Beach, Indonesia

If you like pink, you should seize the opportunity to visit this beach! Pink beaches are very rare – there are only a handful of them in the whole world. The pink colour is caused by tiny red **organisms** that live in the coral reefs. They blend with the white sand to make a pink colour. This pink beach is on Komodo Island in Indonesia.

What else is there to see?

Komodo Island is also famous for its Komodo dragons, which are only found in Indonesia. Komodo dragons are the heaviest lizards on Earth. These powerful predators can eat animals as large as themselves in one go! Komodo dragons also have venomous bites. This means it is very bad news for any animal bitten by a Komodo dragon. Even if they manage to get away, they are still likely to die from the bite.

Shell Beach, Australia

From a long way off, this looks like a white, sandy beach. However, visitors to this beach should know what to expect, with a name like 'Shell Beach'. Shell Beach is one of the few beaches in the world where there's not a grain of sand, just billions of shells. This is probably not the place to take your shoes off for a barefoot stroll across the beach!

The shells are from Fragum cockles, and in places they are up to ten metres deep. The water in the bay is twice as salty as the sea. This makes it hard for predators of the Fragum cockles to survive, so the cockles have thrived.

If you went for a dip here, you would find that you float very easily in the sea. This is because the salt makes the water very **dense**. This means that it's easier for objects to float on it.

Volcanic black beach, Iceland

There aren't many black beaches in the world, but that's not the most interesting thing about this beach in Iceland. It looks as if it's covered in shimmering jewels! They're not real jewels, though – they're giant blocks of ice. The sea has carried them here from a melting glacier. The ice is over 1,000 years old!

It's not a good idea to swim on this beach. You'd need to wrap up warm if you did decide to take a dip.

The black beach is at the shore of Iceland's deepest lake. The lake is formed from melting glacier water. Because of global warming, it's getting larger and larger. In fact, it's four times as big as it was in the 1970s.

The lake connects with the sea, so it's a mix of seawater and **freshwater**. This is what gives the lake its unique colour.

What else is there to see?

If you visit Iceland from September to April, you may be lucky and catch a glimpse of the Northern Lights. Picture yourself standing on the volcanic black beach, with your breath forming clouds in the cold air before you. In the sky above is a ghostly mirage of bright lights. They dance through the sky and reflect in the sparkling ice scattered across the beach in front of you.

Our trip is over

We've travelled far and wide in this exploration of our amazing planet. Hopefully, this book has inspired you to see some of these incredible places when you are older.

Would you prefer to delve into dark caves, or trek up high mountains? Perhaps you love spending time in forests, or was your imagination captured by one of the stunning rivers or lakes?

Which places would you choose to visit?

Enjoy every second of exploring our wonderful world!

Bonus
Packing list

Your packing list will depend on:

- where you are going — is it somewhere hot and tropical, or icy and cold?
- when you are going — temperatures can be very different, depending on when you visit
- what you will do — if you plan on hiking up mountains, you may need to take special equipment.

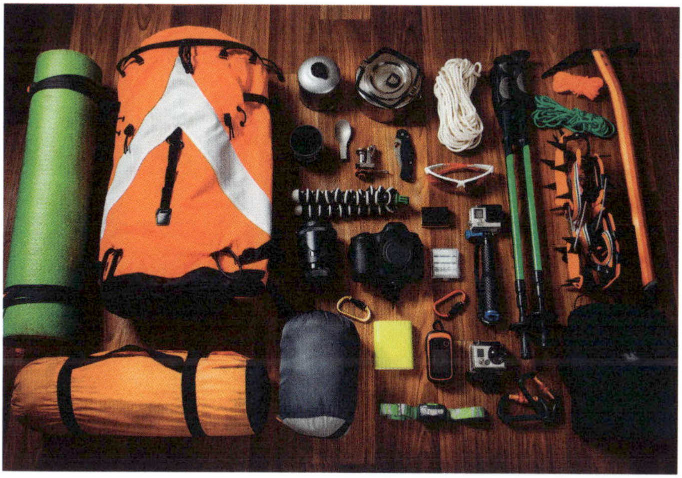

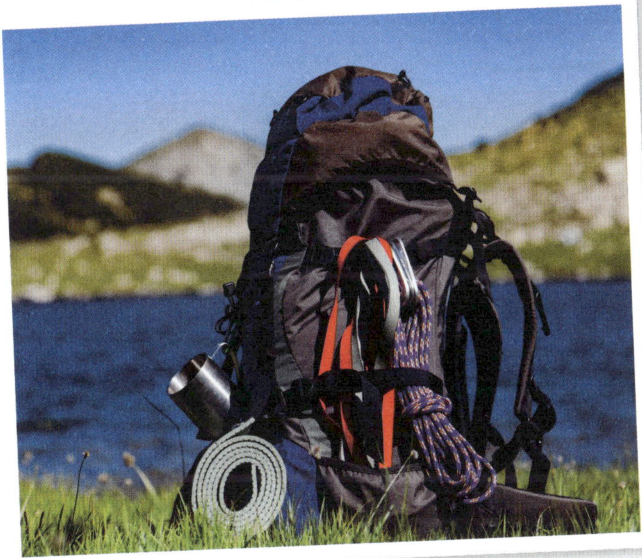

Glossary

bacteria very small living things

crater a large bowl-shaped hole

crystallised turned into crystals

decay rot

dense thick

freshwater natural water that isn't salty

lava rock that is so hot it's become a liquid

magma hot liquid below Earth's crust

marine found in the sea

meteorite a piece of rock that has fallen to Earth from space

minerals things that are naturally made in rocks or earth

mirage when you think you see something in the distance that's not really there

nutrients substances that plants and animals need to live and grow

organisms living things, like animals or plants

ravines deep, narrow valleys with steep sides

uninhabited a place where no one lives

About the author

Why did you want to be a writer?
I loved making up stories as a child. I had a strong imagination and enjoyed thinking of ideas. Then I began to enjoy writing them down – playing around with words, testing how they sounded, what sort of effects I could create.

Abbie Rushton

What's the best thing about writing?
I'm able to visit lots of different places in my imagination. By writing this book, I've imagined myself travelling all over the world, and it was a wonderful adventure!

How do you write a book like this?
I started off with a simple idea of wanting to write about interesting and unusual places around the world – like an alternative tourist guide to less well-known places. Then I did some research into what sort of places I could include and began to organise them into sections, like forests, mountains, deserts.

Why did you want to write this book?
I just love travelling! My first adventure was a round-the-world trip. Since then, I've been very lucky and have visited some truly amazing places around the world.

Have you ever visited any of these places? If so, which one did you like best?

Yes, I've seen the Grand Canyon. I've been in the glow-worm caves in New Zealand, and I've been lucky enough to see the Northern Lights in Iceland. It was the first night of our trip and our flight had been delayed so we were extremely tired. However, we waited up for most of the night to see them. It was worth it!

What was the most interesting thing you learnt from writing this book?

I just loved the fact about the bioluminescent creatures knowing when it's night and day. I was so surprised by that one! I'd also never seen anything like the quartz logs in the Painted Desert. Perhaps I should take a research trip there to find out more!

Is there a place you'd love to visit? Why?

Well, my list is a lot longer after writing this book! There are lots of places in South America in this book, which made me really want to have a long trip there. I've been to Peru and seen lots of the big tourist attractions there, but I missed the Nazca Lines. Maybe I should return to see them, and see more of South America while I'm there.

What do you hope readers will get from the book?

A sense of adventure!

Book chat

Had you ever heard of any of these amazing places before reading this book?

What have you learnt from reading this book?

Have you ever seen anything like the places in the book?

If you could visit one place from this book, where would you choose and why?

What's the fact you found most interesting from the book?

Do you think there may be more amazing places on Earth that we haven't found yet?

If you had to describe this book, what would you say?

Do you think this book would make a good TV show? Why or why not?

If you had to think of a new title for the book, what would it be?

If you could ask the author anything, what would you ask?

Would you recommend this book? Why or why not?

Book challenge:
Create a postcard from any place in this book. How will you draw the place and what will you say about it?

Collins BIG CAT

Published by Collins An imprint of HarperCollins*Publishers*

The News Building
1 London Bridge Street
London
SE1 9GF
UK

Macken House
39/40 Mayor Street Upper
Dublin 1
D01 C9W8
Ireland

Text © Abbie Rushton 2024
Design and illustrations © HarperCollins*Publishers* Limited 2024

10 9 8 7 6 5 4 3 2 1

ISBN 978-0-00-868115-9

All rights reserved. No part of this publication may be reproduced, stored in a retrieval system, or transmitted in any form by any means, electronic, mechanical, photocopying, recording or otherwise, without the prior written permission of the Publisher or a licence permitting restricted copying in the United Kingdom issued by the Copyright Licensing Agency Ltd, 5th Floor, Shackleton House, 4 Battle Bridge Lane, London SE1 2HX.

British Library Cataloguing-in-Publication Data
A catalogue record for this publication is available from the British Library.

Download the teaching notes and word cards to accompany this book at: http://littlewandle.org.uk/signupfluency/

Get the latest Collins Big Cat news at
collins.co.uk/collinsbigcat

Author: Abbie Rushton
Publisher: Laura White
Product manager: Caroline Green
Series editor: Charlotte Raby
Development editor: Catherine Baker
Commissioning editor: Suzannah Ditchburn
Project manager: Emily Hooton
Copyeditor: Sally Byford
Proofreader: Catherine Dakin
Cover designer: Sarah Finan
Typesetter: 2Hoots Publishing Services Ltd
Production controller: Katharine Willard

Printed in the UK.

MIX
Paper | Supporting responsible forestry
FSC™ C007454

This book is produced from independently certified FSC™ paper to ensure responsible forest management.

For more information visit: www.harpercollins.co.uk/green

Made with responsibly sourced paper and vegetable ink

Scan to see how we are reducing our environmental impact.

Acknowledgements
The publishers gratefully acknowledge the permission granted to reproduce the copyright material in this book. Every effort has been made to trace copyright holders and to obtain their permission for the use of copyright material. The publishers will gladly receive any information enabling them to rectify any error or omission at the first opportunity.

p6b Tom Till/Alamy, p7 CaseyWild/Stockimo/Alamy, p11 Petar Belobrajdic/500px/Getty Images, p12 background Stocktrek Images/Getty Images, p13 James Stone/Getty Images, p14t James Stone/Getty Images, p15t Marcel Strelow/Alamy, p15bl Douglas Klug/Getty Images, p17 SinghaphanAllB/Getty Images, p18 imageBROKER.com GmbH & Co. KG/Alamy, p19b Panther Media GmbH/Alamy, p23 MehmetO/Alamy, p27 Travelpix Ltd/Getty Images, p28b Brian Pollard/Alamy, p29 B.O'Kane/Alamy, p31 Javier Trueba/MSF/Science Photo Library, p32 © Alexander Van Driessche, p37b Thomas Janisch/Getty Images, p38 Francesco Riccardo Iacomino/Getty Images, p39b NASA Image Collection/Alamy, p40 Image Source/Getty Images, p41l Minden Pictures/Alamy, p45t Daniel Prudek/Alamy, p46 Lawrence Rigby Latin America/Alamy, p56 Ferrantraite/Getty Images, p57 Westend61 GmbH/Alamy, p60 Ingo Oeland/Alamy, p61 Hilke Maunder/Alamy, p63 Image Professionals GmbH/Alamy, p69 imageBROKER.com GmbH & Co. KG/Alamy. All other photos, Shutterstock.